City Safari

Rat

Isabel Thomas

Raintree

Raintree is an Imprint of Capstone Global Library Limited, a company incorporated in England and Wales having its registered office at 7 Pilgrim Street, London, EC4V 6LB – Registered company number: 6695582

www.raintreepublishers.co.uk
myorders@raintreepublishers.co.uk

Text © Capstone Global Library Limited 2014
First published in hardback in 2014
The moral rights of the proprietor have been asserted.

Edited by Dan Nunn, Rebecca Rissman, and Helen Cox Cannons
Designed by Tim Bond
Original illustrations © Capstone Global Library Ltd 2014
Picture research by Mica Brancic
Production by Helen McCreath
Originated by Capstone Global Library Ltd
Printed and bound in China

ISBN 978 1 406 27126 3
17 16 15 14 13
10 9 8 7 6 5 4 3 2 1

British Library Cataloguing in Publication Data
A full catalogue record for this book is available from the British Library.

Acknowledgements
We would like to thank the following for permission to reproduce photographs: Alamy pp. 6 (© David J Slater), 15 (© Arterra Picture Library/De Meester Johan), 23 pest (© Graham Harrison); Ardea pp. 16 & 23 predator (both © Ardea London); FLPA pp. 10 & 14 (both Erica Olsen), 17 (Martin B Withers); Getty Images pp. 12 (Minden Pictures/Derek Middleton), 21 (Picture Press/Gisela Delpho); Naturepl. com pp. 4 (© Paul Hobson), 5 (© Stephen Dalton), 8 (© Dave Bevan), 11 (© ARCO), 13 (© Colin Preston), 19 (© Dave Bevan), 20 (© Stephen Dalton); Shutterstock pp. 9 & 23 sense (both © Oleg Kozlov), 23 crop (© Sergey Lavrentev), 23 grains (© Svetlana Lukienko); SuperStock pp. 7 (BSIP/Lenartowski), 18 & 23 gnaw (both Biosphoto).
Front cover photograph of a rat reproduced with permission of Shutterstock (© anatolypareev). Back cover photograph of a rat's face reproduced with permission of Shutterstock (© Oleg Kozlov).

We would like to thank Michael Bright for his assistance in the preparation of this book.

Every effort has been made to contact copyright holders of material reproduced in this book. Any omissions will be rectified in subsequent printings if notice is given to the publisher.

Warning!

Never touch wild animals or their homes. Some wild animals carry diseases. Scared animals may bite or scratch you. Never touch rat droppings, or food that rats have been eating.

Note about spotter icon

3

Your eyes, ears, and nose can tell you if a rat is nearby. Look for these clues as you read the book, and find out more on page 22.

Contents

Some words are shown in bold, **like this**.
You can find them in the glossary on page 23.

Who has been caught raiding the rubbish?

small ears

thick fur

tail same length as body

brown rat

Brown fur. Beady eyes. A hairless tail. It's a rat!

Towns and cities are not just home to people and pets.

black rat

large ears

black or brown fur

tail longer than body

Towns and cities are full of wild animals, too.

Come on a city safari. Find out if wild rats are living near you.

Why do rats live in towns and cities?

Wherever people live, rats live, too.

Towns and cities are full of warm places to shelter.

Rats really like rubbish dumps, sewers, houses, and gardens.

In these places, it is easy to find food that people have thrown away.

What makes rats good at living in towns and cities?

Rats are very good at keeping out of sight.

They hide during the day and come out at night.

Rats **sense** food and danger using their paws, whiskers, and noses.

They are clever, and never forget where food can be found.

Where do rats hide during the day?

Brown rats live in large groups in basements, garages, and sewers.

They also dig burrows in gardens and underneath buildings.

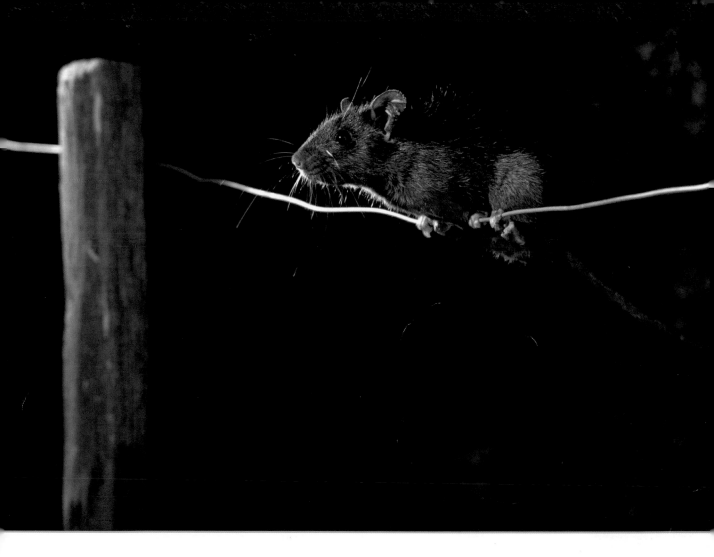

Black rats are good at climbing.

They live high up, inside the roofs and walls of buildings.

What do rats eat?

Rats eat lots of different foods.

They catch small animals, such as baby birds, mice, lizards, and frogs.

They eat things they find, such as fruit and roots.

Rats especially like **grains** and meat.

Why do rats like living near people?

Rats use their amazing **sense** of smell to find food in our rubbish.

They also like to eat food that has not been thrown away!

Rats squeeze into houses and other places where food is stored.

They **gnaw** packets of food and sacks of **grain** open.

What dangers do rats face in towns and cities?

City rats are safe from countryside **predators** such as hawks.

They are hunted by pet dogs and cats, and other rats.

People also trap and kill rats because they are **pests**.

Most city rats die before they are one or two years old.

Why don't people like living near rats?

Rats damage buildings by **gnawing** their way inside.

They eat human and animal food and **crops**.

They damage stored food by weeing and pooing on it.

Rats and their droppings can carry dangerous diseases.

Where are baby rats born?

Baby rats are born in nests inside the rats' hidden homes.

Mother rats share nests and look after the babies together.

Baby rats grow very quickly.

When they are three months old, they are ready to have their own babies.

Rat spotter's guide

Look back at the sights, sounds, and smells that tell you a rat might be nearby. Use these clues to go on your own city safari.

1 A strong, stinky smell can be a sign that rats live in a building. In gardens, they live under compost heaps, sheds, or piles of wood.

2 Rats love to **gnaw**. They leave big tooth marks on wood, plastic, and food containers.

3 Long, thin droppings near food are a sign that rats have visited.

4 Is it a rat or a mouse? Adult rats are much bigger than mice. Young rats might be mouse-sized, but they have much larger heads and feet.

Picture glossary

 **crop** plants grown for food, such as cereal, fruit, and vegetables

 **gnaw** bite or nibble something over and over again

 **grains** seeds of plants such as wheat and corn, which are grown for food

 **pest** animal that causes damage to people's belongings, homes, or to other buildings

 **predator** animal that hunts other animals for food

 **sense** find out what is around through sight, hearing, smell, taste, and touch

Find out more

Books

Wild Read: Rats, Jan Mark
(Oxford University Press, 2009)

Wild Town, Mike Dilger (A & C Black, 2012)

Websites

www.bbc.co.uk/nature/life/brown_rat

Find out more about brown rats on the BBC website.

www.rspca.org.uk/allaboutanimals/pets/rodents/rats

The RSPCA website has lots of information about rats.

Index